INCEST IN MEDIEVAL LITERATURE

Richard J. Warren

Incest in Medieval Literature

Literary depictions of incest from Beowulf to Shakespeare

Richard J. Warren

Muddy Pig Press • Las Vegas, Nevada

Richard J. Warren

Photo Credit: © Can Stock Photo Inc. / Nejron

ISBN-13: 978-0692732823

ISBN-10: 0692732829

Printed in the United States of America

www.muddypigpress.com

Muddy Pig Press • Las Vegas, Nevada

She married. O, most wicked speed, to post

With such dexterity to incestuous sheets!

    – Hamlet (1.2 161-62)

Richard J. Warren

Acknowledgments

Creating a work such as this requires many hands. I would like to thank Dr. Philip Rusche of the University of Nevada, Las Vegas for his assistance with the research and for sharing his extensive knowledge of medieval literature. I would also like to thank Dr. Anne Stevens and Dr. Maile Chapman, both also from UNLV, I could not possibly have completed this project without their ever-present encouragement and support.

Richard J. Warren

Table of Contents

Richard J. Warren

Chapter 1
Introduction

Storytelling serves as a vehicle to guide readers
through a confusing maze of societal expectations that
often contradict the realities faced by the population as a
whole. Considered a universal more of a civilized society
today, the prohibition of incest in medieval Europe may
not have been such a universally accepted principle.
Whether from ignorance of the possible genetic
consequences of incestuous offspring or the simple
necessity of finding a marriage partner, incest occurred
with some degree of regularity as indicated by court
documents from the period. The practice also spawned
an abundance of cautionary tales seen in a variety of
texts, both religious and secular. These texts serve as one
of the few windows to the sexual practices and attitudes
of the medieval populace.

Since the story of Lot or the inadvertent incest of Sophocles' *Oedipus Rex,* nearing or crossing borders of consanguinity occurs with some frequency in early literature. Depictions of the incest taboo existed in the 12th Century writings of Saxo Grammaticus in his *Gesta Danorum* in which Thora commanded her daughter "now of marriageable age" to "defile her father in fornication"[1] and in Geoffrey Chaucer's "The Man of Law's Tale" where "the wicked Canace's example, / Who loved her own brother sinfully."[2] *The Poetic Edda* contained brother-sister incest as did *The Saga of the Volsungs* while *The Saga of King Hrolf Kraki* featured father-daughter relations. The oft debated relationship of Hamlet to his mother Gertrude serves as a later example, though that play contained a significantly clearer, and much less debatable, incidence of incest that often remains overlooked by those obsessed with the implications of the mother-son relationship. Clearly a fascination with readers, incest surfaced as a prominent motif in literature and legend throughout the Anglo-Saxon and medieval

---

[1] Gesta Danourm

[2] Chaucer p. 122

periods and continued into the Renaissance.

Quite often these stories served as cautionary parables while others recounted legendary events and relationships. In some cases an issue exists with regard to clarity of the written words. The Old English poem *Beowulf* contains a number of defective lines, perhaps intentionally altered by a Christian scribe cognizant of pressure from the Church, and their interpretation affects the reading and meaning of the poem. Incest, a clearly visible element in many of the Norse sagas, remains below the surface in *Beowulf*. These incest narratives provide a view of family and kinship and the complicated sexual relationships contained within the family structure of the time.

The sociological conditions in Anglo-Saxon England and the substantial clash of cultures created difficulty in adhering to the stringent rules of the Church. In her seminal work, *Incest and the Medieval Imagination,* Elizabeth Archibald maintained that the, "universal law prohibiting incest was in fact socially constructed, and thus open to interpretation and alteration by the Church authorities." The blending of peoples and cultures with differing views of kinship and marriage remained problematic for Christians attempting to convert the pagan populace and "the confusion was augmented by the fact that there were two very different systems (Christian and pagan) of calculating relationships."[3] The Church, however, seemed more concerned with incest as it related to endogamy rather than with interfamily relationships as a form of sexual abuse.

The writings of the period reflected the intermingling of cultures and the complex evolution in relational boundaries among Christians and Pagans. Archibald states that, "Medieval incest stories are so numerous that it is impossible even to mention them all."[4] The common appearance of incest in literature and the proliferation of consanguinity regulations suggest a frequency of occurrence among the Anglo-Saxon population. Christian authors produced many of these incest narratives, perhaps as a warning to church members or as a critique to their habits or family life. Archibald agrees with this hypothesis saying, "The

---

[3] Archibald p. 27-28

frequent use of the incest theme by clerical writers shows that incestuous desire was not regarded as a rare and barbaric perversion but rather as a common danger for all, rich and poor, powerful and humble, male and female."[5]

   Beowulf contains a passage thought of as incestuous by some, innocent by others, "...and a daughter, I have heard, who was Onela's Queen / a balm in the bed to the battle-scarred Swede."[6] The interpretation of that passage affects the reading and meaning of the poem. Was the poet mindful of his Christian audience in suppressing the nature of an illicit union that crossed the boundaries of consanguinity? Was he unaware of the nature of the relationship? Did the incest occur at all? A material defect in the line obscures the certainty of any explanation in regards to *Beowulf* though incest narratives proliferated in medieval storytelling. *Beowulf* and *The Saga of King Hrolf Kraki* illustrate the substantial difference in the author's treatment of incest in the Norse Sagas and the Anglo-

---

[4] Archibald p. 2
[5] Archibald p. 7
[6] Heaney p. 7

Saxon poem.

Incest provides a necessary ingredient for many creation stories and myths. In the Book of Genesis Adam and Eve famously beget Cain and Abel. Other children, unnamed except for Seth, followed including at least two daughters. Though not explicitly stated, Cain and Abel married their own sisters since no other women existed. Therefore, in the Christian world at least, incest existed since the beginning of time. Later in Genesis Noah and his family reestablish the human race as Noah and his three sons and their wives sire children that form a new civilization. After the birth of those children the proximity of blood relations necessitated close cousins marrying and producing children. The situation required several generations of offspring before its incestuous nature could resolve itself. Also in Genesis, the story of Lot contained father-daughter incest with the two daughters initiating the incident.[7]

Though most biblical references to incest appear in the Old Testament at least one reference exists in the New Testament. The apostle Paul perceived that the

---

[7] King James Bible

Corinthian Church needed to correct problems
concerning their actions. The following passage appears
in Paul's letter to the Corinthians:

> It is reported commonly that there is
> fornication among you, and such
> fornication as is not so much as named
> among the Gentiles, that one should have
> his father's wife. And ye are puffed up,
> and have not rather mourned, that he that
> hath done this deed might be taken away
> from among you.[8]

The letter describes mother-son incest and the tense
suggests that multiple offenders existed rather than a
single perpetrator. The mention in the New Testament
indicates that incest occurred beyond the time needed
for the development of the human race.

In addition to the Bible, depictions of incest exist
in many examples of religious literature. Dante's *Inferno*,
the first book of the *Divine Comedy*, tells the story of
Paolo and Francesca in Canto V. Dante and Virgil meet a
woman, Francesca, who tells them of her sin and reason

---

[8] King James Bible - Corinthians 5.1

for being in hell's second circle. While sitting with her brother-in-law Paolo and reading the Arthurian tale of Lancelot and Guinevere's adulterous tryst, she and Paolo succumbed to their own lustful feelings. The Church considered sexual relations with an in-law a form of incest so Francesca and Paolo found themselves condemned to hell for their actions. Of note, the deeper in hell a sinner resides reflects the seriousness of their transgression so the couple's actions placed them in the second circle indicates that Dante did not deem incest with an in-law as severe a sin as other crimes such as murder.[9] *The Divine Comedy* referenced the adulterous relationship of Lancelot and Guinevere but Arthurian literature contained a number of incestuous situations which will be examined in Chapter 5.

Canto XXX of Dante's *Inferno* illustrated a more severe form of incest as this transgression resulted in condemnation to hell's eighth circle. On his journey downward Dante encountered Myrrha, a princess from Greek mythology. Myrrha's grave sin was to engage in sexual relations with her own father, as a consequence

---

[9] Dante 31

she suffered a fate far worse than Francesca and Paolo. Myrrha's incest was that of deception in that after falling in love with him she tricked her father into engaging in intercourse by pretending that she was someone else.[10] Her punishment consisted to being transformed into a tree and gave birth to Adonis while in this form.

Many of the incest stories found in medieval literature derived from works written in antiquity. The well-known story of *Oedipus Rex* failing to recognize his own mother appears in various forms. (The failure to recognize one's kin occurs with frequency in these stories and such incest seems excusable when the perpetrators do not understand that the relationship between them.) The Greek tale of *Apollonius of Tyre* reappears in Gower's *Confessio Amantis* and Shakespeare's *Pericles, Prince of Tyre*. Canace from Greek mythology appears in Ovid's *Heroides* and reappears in Gower's *Confessio Amantis* as well as "Chaucer's Man of Law's Tale." The retelling of classical stories comes as no surprise. As Archibald points out, "Medieval readers would have been well aware of the rich mythographic and commentary

---

[10] Dante 145

tradition on classical texts."[11] Familiarity with the stories from which medieval tales derived provide a level of comfort for readers making it easier to connect with the message provided by the author, a fact the authors likely understood.

Another aspect of incest in mythology and Norse literature concerned hero warriors. Many, such as Hrolf Kraki, were the product of an incestuous union. While the medieval Christian writers portrayed incestuous couplings as something that invited condemnation from God, the subject received different treatment in the Norse sagas. While the exact reason for the disparity remains unclear, cultural aspects perhaps play a role. The pagan writers, whether due to circumstance or simply attitude, do not seem to view incest through the same negative lens, though that's not meant to suggest that the view is favorable. These texts will be examined in Chapter 6.

The incest motif continued beyond the medieval period and into the Renaissance, appearing in plays by William Shakespeare, John Ford and Christopher

---

[11] Archibald 53

Marlowe. The popularity of incest plays and narratives during the Renaissance reflect a changing social dynamic. Archibald points out that, "In Renaissance incest plays the focus is no longer on individual souls, but on society more generally."[12] The transition from the Middle Ages to the Renaissance saw the change from incest being viewed as an individual sin to a more generalized societal taboo. That's not to suggest incest was no longer viewed as an egregious offense but more of a societal ill. Quite the contrary, incest remained a crime as evidenced by the fact that one of the charges brought against Ann Boleyn was that of sodomy with her own brother. Though the charge may have been untrue, the fact that it existed shows that incest still held sway as a serious offense in the Renaissance.

---

[12] Archibald 235-36

Richard J. Warren

Chapter 2
Sexuality & Incest

Although few Anglo-Saxon and other medieval texts survive, what remains often serves as the only window into the workings of medieval society. In *Sexuality in Medieval Europe* Ruth Mazo Karras states that, "Literary sources can be among the most useful sources for the history of sexuality because (in the absence of private letters) imaginative literature gives us the most vivid examples of actual medieval life."[13] Though mostly unnamed, the vast majority of authors exhibited a strong Christian ideology, not surprising in light of significant Church influence at the time. Certainly no tome such as *The Joy of Sex* nor a *Kinsey Report* on human sexuality exist for the time but much

---

[13] Karras 10

information of medieval sexuality and prevailing attitudes exists in the writings of the period. Some overtly stated information appears while much more remains buried within subtleties in need of interpretation. In their collection of academic essays, *Sexual Culture in the Literature of Medieval Britain*, Robert Allen Rouse and Cory James Rushton state that, "The sexual culture of medieval Britain was diverse and complex, both in its manifestation in theory and practice, and in the uses to which it was deployed in the literary remains from the period."[14] Those literary remnants often represent the only evidence of medieval sexuality in existence. Sifting through the texts and decoding sometimes obscure references often requires making inferential leaps without sufficient corroboration in an effort to ascertain the proclivities of the medieval population.

Sexual themes flourished in the writings medieval Europe. Indeed, Foucault stated the "Middle Ages had organized around a theme of the flesh."[15] In

[14] Rouse

[15] Foucault 33

literature that hardly represented a new phenomenon, but rather a continuation of one that existed since antiquity. Greek, Roman and Norse mythology each featured sexual themes as did classical literature. The subset of incest traveled in lockstep with those of adultery, rape and other forms of sexual deviance from the time of antiquity through the Renaissance and beyond. The themes and their popularity likely reflected the attitudes and experiences of the population since authors tend to produce material their audience desires.

The commonality of incest stories highlighted not only their popularity, but the frequency with which incest occurred among the medieval population. The notion that the writings simply depict fictional fantasy is refuted by hard evidence. Kathryn Gravdal researched court records for indications of crimes relating to incest. She uncovered numerous accounts where incest served as a given defense:

> ... it is in the criminal legislation of
> infanticide that medieval records reveal
> the existence of sexual abuses by family
> members. In studying the records of

infanticide trials and pardon letters for
women convicted of this crime, one
discovers repeated mentions of incest
within the nuclear family. It is not
uncommon that the reason a woman gives
for infanticide is that the pregnancy was a
result of intercourse with her father,
grandfather, or brother. Thus we can be
certain that the sexual abuse of children
and adolescents by adult relatives did in
fact occur in medieval French society.[16]

Of note, the charges did not include incest. Gravdal
adds, "Significantly, such infanticide narratives censure
(or pardon) the perpetrator of infanticide for her crime,
but not the perpetrator of incest for his crime."[17] Though
certainly viewed as a sin by the Church and a crime
under the vernacular law, the patriarchal nature of
medieval society allowed the male offenders to escape
punishment.

---

[16] Gravdal 282

[17] Gravdal 282

Much like the case of Adam and Eve, the tendency to place blame upon the female offender in a crime that requires two participants appears in many, though not all, literary depictions of incest. Chaucer mentions "the wicked Canace" but not her brother Macareus as if she alone deserves blame for their incestuous union. Other such cases will appear in subsequent chapters. Not all incestuous relationships deserve blame since some of the incidents occur inadvertently.

Many medieval incest plotlines revolve around a lack of recognition between the offending parties. The variation derives for the story of Oedipus where he kills his father and unknowingly marries his mother. The lack of recognition does not absolve guilt as there are consequences to be paid. In the case of Oedipus he suffered the loss of his kingdom and felt compelled to blind himself after his wife/mother committed suicide. In some case the recognition occurs prior to sex taking place, thereby averting the sin. This is true of Gawain of the Arthurian legends which be examined in Chapter 5.

A case of inadvertent incest due to a lack of recognition occurs in *The Saga of King Hrolf Kraki.* The saga's central female character Yrsa, herself the product of a troubled relationship and the rape of Queen Ólaf by her father Helgi, does not know the nature of her conception. Thirteen years later she meets and falls in love with Helgi unaware of his role in her birth. When the two wed Yrsa has married her own father. The incestuous union begets a son, Hrolf, the hero of the saga. When Queen Ólaf informs her daughter that she inadvertently married her own father Yrsa immediately decides she cannot remain in the marriage. Her reaction indicates the lack of acceptance of incest, "I shall not stay here, now that I know what shame lies over us."[18] Incestuous liaisons seem to occur with greater frequency in Norse literature than they do in Anglo-Saxon tales but that does not indicate the acceptance of the practice as evidenced by Yrsa's reaction. A paradox exists, however, in that children born of incest, such as Hrolf, often emerge as larger-than-life heroes.

The intentional act of incest does not always

---

[18] Kraki 59

involve awareness of both parties. Several stories exist of
one person using deceit, such as the case of Myrrha
tricking her father into having intercourse, or magic to
engage the other unawares. In the in *Saga of the Volsungs*
Signý enlists the aid of a sorceress to disguise herself in
order to have sex with her twin brother Sigmund,
begetting their son, Sinfjötli.[19] We will see later in the
Arthurian tale *Cligés* a case of magic used to deceive
another into believing that sex had taken place when it
clearly did not. Though the act that failed to occur did
not constitute incest, the magic did permit another of
incest by affinity to take place.

Variations exist in the structure of incestuous
relationships. Sibling incest generally occurs in the form
of opposite sex, rarely same sex pairings. Father-
daughter and mother-son couplings occur frequently in
both the intentional and inadvertent form. The father
generally initiates acts with his daughter though some
cases, such as Lot and his daughters or Myrrha and her
father, are initiated by the child partner. Another
variation involves a daughter fleeing a father either after

---

[19] Volsung Saga

incest or prior to its occurrence with the male depicted as domineering. The patriarchal nature of medieval society, the concept of a daughter being the father's property and the lack of a specific prohibition, Biblical or laic, against the practice of father-daughter incest may account for the proliferation of stories involving this pairing and indicate that it likely represented a not uncommon occurrence.

The frequency of incest stories seems more abundant in Norse literature than in English literature of the period. Though this perhaps indicates a greater degree of acceptance, or at least some level of tolerance, of the practice, the pagan culture did not necessarily approve of it. Helen Damico notes that pagans as well as Christians viewed the occurrence incest as an unacceptable practice in their respective societies and states that, "For incest, because it betrays troth within the family, strikes at the core of society – whether Christian or pagan... an embodiment of social evil."[20] The propensity to treat children of incest, such as Hrolf Kraki, as heroes, however, provides for a positive

---

[20] Damico 177

outcome to and act thought to violate social mores.

A combination of many factors likely led to the proliferation of incest in the medieval society of Europe. The lack of awareness in regard to genetic consequences removes one barrier to incest. People living in close quarters with little or no privacy combined with raw sexual desire create temptations which Augustine called "the morbid condition of lust"[21] that proved difficult for some to overcome. The necessity of finding a mate in a sparse population provides another excuse for overlooking the prohibitions against relationships that violate consanguinity protocols. The patriarchal nature of a society that viewed women as property and provided little legal protection for them allows for the dismissing of a daughter's right to refuse her father if he harbored incestuous desires. That's not to suggest that men routinely ravished their daughters, just that some might use the lack of a legal prohibition as justification. Absent any official historical documentation, the nature of medieval sexuality, and manifestations of incest, must be deciphered from the literary depictions that survive.

---

[21] Rouse 7

Richard J. Warren

Chapter 3

Affinity Regulations

The Bible stands as the basis of Church regulations and edicts found in Leviticus 18 enumerated restrictions regarding consanguineous sexual relations. "None of you shall approach to any that is near of kin to him, to uncover their nakedness,"[22] stated the most basic admonition. Many prohibitions ensued including "the nakedness of thy mother, shalt thou not uncover: she is thy mother; thou shalt not uncover her nakedness."[23] Fornication between siblings, grandchildren, aunts, uncles, cousins, in-laws and step-children or parents met with the same restrictions. The notable absences from these laws concern sex between a father and daughter.

---

[22] Leviticus 18:6
[23] Leviticus 18:7

The assumption that such a restriction exists by convention is refuted by specificity of Leviticus 18. Medieval views of a female child's status dictated that a man's daughter remains his property until her betrothal to another; if those rights extend to those of the flesh then the manifestations of incest in literature could exist as a way to question the wisdom of such policy. Allusions to incest imply that such liaisons occurred with sufficient frequency to, at the very least, warrant discussion of the possibility.

In A.D. 597 Pope Gregory dispatched Augustine of Canterbury to England on a mission to convert the isle's inhabitants to Christianity. Augustine encountered difficulty with the pagan population's propensity for affinity marriage in degrees closer than the seven proscribed by the Church. In need of guidance, Augustine requested clarification from Pope Gregory in regard to the consanguinity protocol by posing the question, "To what degree may the faithful marry with their kindred?"[24] Pope Gregory's reply:

---

[24] Bede   79-80

> …an earthly law of the Roman state
> permits first-cousins to marry. But
> experience shows that such unions do not
> result in children, and sacred law forbids
> a man to *"uncover the nakedness of his
> kindred."* Necessity therefore forbids a
> closer marriage than between the third or
> fourth generation, while the second
> generation, as we have said, should
> wholly abstain from marriage.[25]

Gregory's acceptance of marriage as close as the third or
fourth generation represents a departure from the
Church's official position of seven generations of
separation.[26] Pagan tradition or a simple proclivity for
close marriage combined with a lack of population
density likely necessitated such a shift. The revised
protocols of Pope Gregory would not become official
Church policy until the Fourth Lateran Council of 1215.

In the Papal decrees of Gregory little distinction
exists between sexual relations involving consanguinity,

---

[25] Bede   80

[26] Archibald 28

affinity by marriage, spiritual affinity and those within the nuclear family itself. The lack of specificity serves to distort boundaries treating sex with blood relations and close, non-blood affinity resulting from marriage as equally sinful. In her essay "Confessing Incests," Kathryn Gravdal states, "the single category of incest blurs and erases the great differences between marriage within the tribe and sex within the family."[27] The Church's omission of detail regarding certain blood relations could also imply that occurrence within the nuclear family unit rarely took place and the issue was not considered serious enough to warrant inclusion. Gravdal asserts that assumption would be incorrect, "If twentieth-century scholars were to read church law alone, we might assume that incest within the nuclear family did not exist or that it was not understood to be a sin. Both assumptions would be incorrect."[28] The English law and later penitential guides that followed Gregory's edicts did include some more specific references to incest within the immediate family though the lines between

[27] Gravdal 280

[28] Gravdal p. 281

nuclear relations and close affinity remained indistinct.

In addition to Gregory's papal decrees rooted in Leviticus, secular law in England placed prohibitions on sexual relations. King Æthelbert's seventh-century Kentish laws listed penalties for certain adulterous acts but omitted incestual relationships. The laws indicate that a maiden belongs to a man, presumably her father. Though not evidence of connubial privilege, rights of ownership of a father over daughter clearly exist. How far those rights extend remains a matter of conjecture.

The consanguinity doctrines of Theodore of Tarsus, seventh-century Archbishop of Canterbury, provided the clergy with clarification of the Church's position on sexual relations among parishioners. The *Canons of Theodore* did include provisions for incestuous relations within the nuclear family and proscribed the appropriate penance for various infractions:

> If anyone takes his own kinsman in
> marriage, or the woman whom his near-
> kinsman had (in marriage) before, let him
> be excommunicated.
> If anyone fornicates with his mother, he

must fast for 15 years and never change that except on Sunday alone.

If a brother fornicates with his natural brother through the mingling of their bodies, he must fast for 15 winters without meat.

If a mother fornicates with her little son, she must not taste meat for 3 years and fast 1 day in the week up to eventide.

Whoever fornicates with his sister is to fast for 12 winters.

Whoever fornicates with his mother must fast for 15 years and never change that except on Sunday and in holy times; and also he is to journey to foreign lands and fast for 7 years.

Whoever fornicates with his sister must fast for 7 years.[29]

Theodore's Canons and penitential codes existed to guide clergy in proscribing the appropriate penance to those committing sins of the flesh. The canons address

---

[29] Frantzen np

homosexuality, sexual conduct between siblings, and mother-child incest. Congruent with the early English Laws and Leviticus, no mention of father-daughter relations exist in the canons. Gravdal commented on this omission, "It is striking that there is no mention of the possibility of incest committed by the father."[30] She emphasizes that penitential laws mention transgressions committed by the mother more than once. Though intriguing by their absence, such exclusion of prohibitions for the father, however, fails to confirm the endorsement of a father-daughter incestual relationship.

The first appearance of any regulation of incest in English secular law appears in the ninth-century laws of King Alfred:

> And in the case of incestuous unions, the
> councilors have decided that the king
> shall take possession of the male offender,
> and the bishop the female offender, unless
> they make compensation before God and
> the world as the bishop shall prescribe, in

---

[30] Gravdal p. 282

accordance with the gravity of the

offense.[31]

The wording assumes a heterosexual liaison and, unlike Leviticus, homosexual incest remains unstated.

Significant Papal influence and the Biblical origin of the doctrines allow for expectations of similarity between penitential code and English law. The intricate details of the references to incest may imply regularity of occurrence of relationships closer than those allowed and the need for regulation of the degrees of consanguineal separation in marriage. Archibald states that the appearance of incest in literature occurred because it also existed in the population and concludes that:

> The literature of the period also suggests
> that incest occurred quite frequently. If it
> had been extremely rare, it would have
> been bad propaganda for the Church to
> make a showpiece of the contrition of
> incestuous sinners.[32]

---

[31] Attenborough p. 105

[32] Archibald p. 231

The protocols existed out of the necessity for controlling incest and went beyond blood relations. The regulations prohibited marriage between in-laws on the premise that the act of marital intercourse created one flesh. The Church's meticulous attention paid to the issue of incest signified its importance and raised awareness which probably led to the inclusion of the incest motif in literary works.

Despite the influence of the Church and the prospect of eternal damnation, the marriage laws that existed in theory often went ignored in reality. Archibald explained that ignorance of the laws played a role:

> Plenty of people seem to have ignored the
> rules on of incest in the broader sense;
> though some were brought to court, the
> evidence of the many decrees, the
> ecclesiastical correspondence, and the
> manuals about confession and penance
> suggest that many people broke the laws
> with impunity, and without guilty
> consciences whether through ignorance of

the law or of precise degrees of
relationship.[33]

The inhabitants of Anglo-Saxon England lived primarily
on farms or in small villages, and travel outside of their
immediate area was difficult and often dangerous. Such
proximity may foster a sense of community and
reinforce the bonds of kinship but it also left fewer
choices regarding marriage partners. The lack of options
combined with Church affinity rules that remained
stricter than their Pagan counterparts exacerbated the
issue. Archibald stated "the prohibited degrees of
relationship grew to the point where most people living
in small communities could not legally marry anyone
they knew."[34]

Evidence of nuclear family incest exists in
abundance. As stated earlier, Gravdal explored incidents
of infanticide in medieval France as an indication of
familial sexual abuse:

...it is in the criminal legislation of
infanticide that medieval records reveal

---

[33] Archibald p. 46

[34] Archibald p. 41

the existence of sexual abuse by family
members...It is not uncommon that the
reason a woman gives for infanticide is
that the pregnancy was a result of
intercourse with her father, grandfather,
or brother.... we can be certain that sexual
abuse of children and adolescents by
adult relatives did in fact occur .[35]

Literary depictions of incest allow for their interpretation
as fictional cautionary tales but Gravdal shows that legal
records provide irrefutable evidence of occurrence.
Gravdal also includes a note on culpability,
"Significantly, such incest narratives censure (or pardon)
the perpetrator of infanticide for her crime, but not the
perpetrator of incest for his crime."[36] That the female
victim bears the burden of responsibility provides more
evidence of the patriarchal nature of medieval society.

Pope Innocent III convened the Fourth Lateran
Council in 1215 which significantly relaxed the
consanguinity and affinity regulations. Marriage within

---

[35] Gravdal p. 282

[36] Gravdal p. 282

four degrees of affinity became permissible. Canon 50 states:

> ...the prohibition against marriage shall not in future go beyond the fourth degree of consanguinity and of affinity, since the prohibition cannot now generally be observed to further degrees without grave harm.... Although the prohibition of marriage is now restricted to the fourth degree, we wish the prohibition to be perpetual, notwithstanding earlier decrees on this subject issued either by others or by us.[37]

Two additional canons further clarified rules pertaining to marriage. Canon 51 forbade clandestine marriages. Prior to the relaxation of affinity regulations that banned marriage within seven degrees of affinity people often engaged in clandestine unions, both with intent and due to ignorance, that circumvented the regulations. The Church decreed that the relaxed protocols required strict adherence to the new four degree mandate. Those in

---

[37] Papal Encyclicals (Canon 50)

violation suffered the consequences:

> If any persons presume to enter into
> clandestine marriages of this kind, or
> forbidden marriages within a prohibited
> degree, even if done in ignorance, the
> offspring of the union shall be deemed
> illegitimate and shall have no help from
> their parents' ignorance, since the parents
> in contracting the marriage could be
> considered as not devoid of knowledge,
> or even as affecters of ignorance.[38]

Consequences also existed for priests who performed prohibited marriages and even clergy who simply attended the ceremony. Additionally the canon cautioned against making a false claim that a marriage violates the rules stating, "Anybody who maliciously proposes an impediment, to prevent a legitimate marriage, will not escape the church's vengeance."[39]

Canon 52 concerned evidence presented at matrimonial trials. Prior to the revision trials allowed the

---

[38] Papal Encyclicals (Canon 51)

[39] Papal Encyclicals (Canon 51)

presentation of hearsay evidence. Attempting to document consanguinity and affinity proved difficult due to "the shortness of human life [where] witnesses would not be able to testify from first-hand knowledge in a reckoning as far as the seventh degree." The new canons decreed that "in future witnesses from hearsay shall not be accepted in this matter, since the prohibition does not now exceed the fourth degree." The canon also allowed for the possibility that a witness might posses an ulterior motive when offering testimony and required that, "The witnesses shall affirm on oath that in bearing witness in the case they are not acting from hatred or fear or love or for advantage."[40]

The relaxed consanguinity and affinity rules brought with them demands for stricter adherence to the regulations as evidenced by the content of Canon 51. Literary evidence suggests that the population often ignored this demand. Post Lateran Council literature contained as much, of not more, of the incest motif.

---

[40] Papal Encyclicals (Canon 52)

Chapter 4
Beowulf

Extensive description of bloodlines and family history in *Beowulf* allow for the detection of relationships that may run afoul of the consanguinity protocols, whether they occurred accidentally or with intent. Though prominent displays of consanguineous relationships, kinship and family lineage existed in *Beowulf* and references to the Scylding dynasty, the Geats and Swedes appear in detail but one familial link remains ambiguous. Controversy surrounds an unnamed queen in *Beowulf* and of her possible identification as the legendary Yrsa of *The Saga of King Hrolf Kraki* and other Norse tales. Such identification creates the possibility for the existence of an incestuous relationship. The focus of the controversy centers on the interpretation of lines 59-63:

> He was four times a father, this fighter
> prince:
> one by one they entered the world,
> Heorogar, Hrothgar, the good Halga
> and a daughter, I have heard, who was
> Onela's queen,
> a balm in the bed to the battle-scarred
> Swede.[41]

Casual reading of this translation reveals that Halfdane
had a daughter who married Onela, though the daughter
remained unnamed. However, disputes in interpretation
occur among critics due to a significant defect in line 62
obfuscating the identity of the prince's female offspring.
In his work, *Heroic Legend and in Current Speech,* Kemp
Malone argued that the woman is Yrsa,[42] from the
Scylding legend, and married to Halga, he bases this
assertion on a complicated case of mistaken identity:

> The English poet was probably mistaken
> in thinking that this Danish king
> [Halfdane] had a daughter; Onela was
> actually married, in my opinion, to

[41] Heaney p. 7

Healfdene's daughter-in-law Yrsa, widow

of Healfdene's son Halga.[43]

Malone's constructs his identification of Yrsa on

evidence found in *Hrolfsaga Kraki* but as James Earl states

"in the saga and other analogues Yrsa is not only Halga's

wife but also his daughter,"[44]an irrefutable description of

father-daughter incest that Malone neglects to mention

in his essay.

Helen Damico discusses Malone's assertion and

explores Yrsa in detail supplying a theory as to the

omission of Yrsa from the *Beowulf* text:

...he [the poet] would have implanted

into the poems thematic structure the

motifs of rape and incest, narrative

features that, on the one hand, might have

made the poem's "Christian author" liable

to censure and, on the other, might have

violated the decorum of a poem whose

focus is heroic virtue and conduct.[45]

Damico states that Malone's argument necessitated the

---

[42] Malone p. 51-52
[43] Malone p. 51
[44] Earl p. 296

poet's awareness of Yrsa's history and states, "the presumption here is the *Beowulf* poet was as privy to the legendary events relating to Yrsa as he was to those regarding the rest of the Scyldings."[46] Damico also suggests that the Church and Christian audience caused the poet to suppress Yrsa's "sexual impropriety" by omitting her identity:

> It is understandable that the
> disapprobation of the Christian secular
> and ecclesiastical communities would
> have impelled him to exercise a measure
> of caution in delineating a figure who had
> committed the worst sins of the flesh. For
> incest, because it betrays troth within the
> family, strikes at the core of society –
> whether Christian or pagan – and Yrsa
> undisguised would have been as flagrant
> a symbol of *luxuria,* an embodiment of
> social evil...[47]

Interestingly Damico portrays incest as an affront to

[45] Damico p. 111
[46] Damico p. 118
[47] Damico p. 177

pagan as well as Christian society even though incest in pagan literature occurs with enough frequency that one could possibly conclude that it may not actually carry such a taint. In addition the claim represents the broad scope of all pagan society disallowing for difference between segments of the culture. Regardless of the outcome of the debate over Yrsa's inclusion in *Beowulf*, her place of kinship in the legends of the Scylding dynasty exists without dispute as does her incestuous role in *The Saga of King Hrolf Kraki*.

In "The Sexual Ideology of Hrólfs Saga Kraka," Carl Phelpstead discusses the saga's treatment of sexual themes including rape and incest and "affirms the text's consistent moral that men's uncontrolled sexual desire for women has harmful social consequences."[48] Yrsa, herself the product of a troubled relationship and the rape of Queen Ólaf by her father Helgi, inadvertently marries her father thirteen years later. The union of Yrsa and Helgi begets a son, Hrolf, the Hrothulf of *Beowulf*. When Queen Ólaf informs her daughter that she inadvertently married her own father Yrsa immediately

---

[48] Phelpstead p. 9

decides she cannot remain in the marriage. Her reaction indicates the lack of acceptance of incest, "I shall not stay here, now that I know what shame lies over us."[49] The reference to shame supports Damico's claim of incest being an affront to pagans.

In the saga Yrsa subsequently marries King Adils but Malone postulates the existence of another marriage of Yrsa occurring after Helgi and before King Adils, thereby making the disputed connection to Onela in *Beowulf*.[50] Absent a resolution of the defective line, that identification remains in dispute. Despite the difficulty, "It is hard to get rid of Yrse and Onela, because those who brood on all the tangled relationships in the poem find a Yrse-Onela marriage more than just a curious possibility."[51]

Intriguingly, though Earl does not overtly agree with Malone's identification, he indicates that it helps to clarify the poem's affinity relationships:

If Onela is married to Hroðgar's sister, the
two ends of the poem are interestingly

---

[49] Kraki p. 59
[50] Malone p. 52
[51] Earl p. 296

> tied together. The link completes the circle
> of personal bonds holding the royal
> houses of the Geats, Swedes, and Danes
> together, with Beowulf at the center,
> related to everyone.[52]

Though *Beowulf* and the *Hrolf Saga Kraki* were written at vastly different times, their connection through related legends seems clear.

Earl suggested that to understand the relationships both between *Beowulf* and *Hrolf Saga Kraki* and within the texts themselves requires a combined deliberation and analysis of the stories:

> An inter-textual reading produces its own
> aesthetic effects. Among these are a finer
> sense of the poem's genre, style, and
> raison d'être and a heightened awareness
> of the spider-webbing connotations of
> what might at first appear to be
> innocuous, ornamental, or arbitrary
> details.[53]

---

[52] Earl p. 296
[53] Earl p. 290

The complexity of the sexual relationships in each work differs significantly. Where Phelpstead points to the unabashed sexual transparency of *Hrólfs Saga Kraka*, Earl says "I sense that the *Beowulf* poet suppressed a number of traditional Germanic elements (rape, incest), probably because given his purposes he found them simply too hot to handle."[54] Though *Kraki* and *Beowulf* were both written subsequent to Christianity's arrival in Europe, they reflect different social mores.

Employing Earl's suggestion of an inter-textual reading of *Beowulf* and the sagas while narrowing the focus to sexual elements assists in the delineation of sexual attitudes depicted in the works. In *Beowulf* the focus remains with the Geat hero and his exploits. If incest and other sexual elements exist, they would be contained in what Earl refers to as the poem's "dark matter we can feel in the poem, even if we cannot see it."[55] The poem rarely makes reference to female figures and sexual conduct, illicit or otherwise, remains unspoken.

---

[54] Earl p. 291
[55] Earl p. 298

In the *Saga of the Volsungs* though Signý disguises herself, no camouflage conceals the incident of her engaging in a sexual act with her brother. The incestual coupling occurred without her brother's knowledge or consent nor did Signý express any remorse for her actions. The narrative contains additional sexual references involving the title character, Volsung, "Now when he reached manhood Hrimnir sent his daughter Hliod to him."[56] Another clear indication of sexual activity involved Signý and King Siggeir, "that night, we are told, Siggeir slept with Signý."[57] Unapologetic sexuality flows through the course of the narrative as shown when Signý's son Sinfjotli "went off raiding again. He saw a good looking woman and desired her very much."[58] Allusions to sexuality common in the saga do not appear in *Beowulf*.

Both *Hrólfs Saga Kraki* and *Saga of the Volsungs*, feature numerous examples of sexuality throughout the work. In addition to the aforementioned rape and incest, sexual elements figure prominently in the text.

---

[56] Volsung Saga p. 3
[57] Volusng Saga p. 5
[58] Volsung Saga P. 18

Phelpstead confirms the theme's importance to the structure of the saga:

> Sexual themes are also prominent in the saga, and they relate to that of strife among kindred both because kinship necessarily has a sexual basis and also because the saga reveals ways in which sexual desire and the transgression of accepted gender roles disrupt and threaten a peacefully ordered society.[59]

Phelpstead stresses the importance of the sexual element in the saga as well as the relationship of the sexual theme to kinship. The element of kinship in Beowulf does not have the same sexual connection exhibited in the saga. Phelpstead concludes that:

> We have seen that sexual activity of various kinds features prominently in *Hrólfs* saga and a critical reading of the saga can reveal characteristics of the sexual ideology and the gender system that inform the narrative. A dominant

---

[59] Phelpstead p. 2

theme of the saga is the tragedy of conflict between kindred, and although social bonds of kinship are established through sexual activity, the familial strife engendered in the saga also often has a sexual basis or origin.[60]

The inclusion of sexual elements in the sagas points to the level of acceptance, or possibly expectations, of the motif by the audience.

The *Beowulf* poet's avoidance of a sexual theme may reflect implied pressure from the Church to avoid inclusion of such an ingredient. Additionally the chance exists of a Christian scribe suppressing such an element. Church influence creating wariness on the part of the poet to feature the incest motif remains a possibility. The poet's fear of antagonizing the Church perhaps extended to the audience possessing a reluctance of hearing such a sinful tale for fear of retribution from God.

The Beowulf character's depiction as a courageous figure in a male-dominated tale of heroic feats presents a more likely explanation for the omission.

---

[60] Phelpstead p. 21

The poet's focus on the protagonist's gallant actions and the paucity of female figures in the poem highlights this excess of masculinity. Rather than a conscious avoidance of incest, the component may simply lack relevance in the male-dominated story.

Though also heroic in nature, the Norse sagas exhibit an undercurrent of sexuality. Female characters appear with frequency and play vital roles. Interrelationships between genders and the associated sexual tensions serve as a fertile landscape for the incest motif. The receptiveness of the saga's audience likely factored in as well. Though based on earlier legends, the sagas appeared several centuries after *Beowulf*. This difference in time is sufficient for prevailing attitudes to experience a significant change. The later audience of the Norse sagas may not have feared the wrath of a vengeful God for simply hearing an incestuous tale.

More than just differing audience expectations for *Beowulf* and the sagas, the dissimilarity of treatment could be based upon genre. Though both could be considered heroic tales, *Beowulf* exists primarily as a heroic epic with a background of kinship and family lineage. The *Saga of the Volsungs* and *Hrólfs Saga Kraki* function principally as tales of ancestral heritage with a heroic element. The genres are closely related but with subtle elemental differences that may explain the disparity of treatment in regard to the incest motif.

Absent irrefutable textual or historical evidence the precise reason for the differences remains indeterminable. Church influence, author discretion, audience expectations and even genre all conceivably influenced the respective authors' purpose and the eventual outcome. Certitude does extend to the considerable distinctions in the treatment of incest between the sagas and *Beowulf,* which illustrate differences in the tales available to their respective audiences.

Richard J. Warren

Chapter 5
Arthurian Eroticism

According to Helen Cooper in her introduction to Sir Thomas Malory's *Le Morte Darthur*, one of the earliest references to King Arthur appeared in *Annales Cambriae* with a report of his death at the battle of Camlann in 537CE, an entry she called "the first that lays claim to historical plausibility."[61] Arthur's existence or lack thereof matters little in terms of the impact of Arthurian romances on medieval literature. Cooper goes on to write that "between that date [of the battle of Calmann], whether legendary or historical, and the first full account of Arthur written 600 years later, legends about him were widespread."[62] Geoffrey of Monmouth wrote that

---

[61] Malory viii

[62] Malory viii

full account of Arthur in *The History of the Kings of Britain*
describing exploits that marked "King Arthur as a figure
of international repute, a British figure to rival the
French Charlemagne or even Alexander the Great."[63]
Though the tales' popularity ebbed and flowed over the
centuries, they provide a glimpse into the sexual
appetites and attitudes of their medieval readership.

Many authors wrote tales based on the Arthurian
legend or made reference to one or more of the stories.
Chaucer's Wife of Bath spoke of King Arthur, *The Pearl*
poet is believed to have written *Sir Gawain and the Green
Knight*, Tennyson wrote of Camelot in *The Lady of Shallot*
while his *Idylls of the King* uses twelve poems to recount
the Arthurian legend, Dante referenced Lancelot and
Guinevere in *The Divine Comedy*. The aforementioned
Geoffrey of Monmouth provided a pseudo-historical
account of Arthur while Chrétien de Troyes wrote
several French versions of the romances. Two centuries
after Chrétien, Malory wrote *Le Morte Darthur* which not
only depicted the death of the legendary king, it moved
the story further than previous versions in terms of

---

[63] Geoffrey 27

sexuality. The proliferation of authors embracing the theme speaks to the reader's appetite for such tales. Cooper states that the tales "were enjoying a new surge of popularity in the fifteenth century, with new manuscript copies being made and a cult of chivalry to encourage their reading."[64]

Arthurian literature appeared in both the French and English language but the type of content found in each varied little. The sexual themes, both subtle and explicit, likely enhanced the popularity of the tales among readers. Arthurian romances featured topics of courtly love and chivalry with knights seeking to woo and impress damsels and win their love with feats of strength and displays of courage. The tales also depicted a much darker side with scenes of violence, rape and incest. The rape of women appeared with startling frequency in tales such as Chaucer's *Wife of Bath's Tale*, Chrétien's *The Knight of the Cart* and *The Knight with the Lion*, and the anonymous *The Weddynge of Sir Gawen and Dame Ragnelle* and *The Marriage of Sir Gawain*. In her essay "Invisible Women," Amy Vines stated, "the act or

---

[64] Malory ix

threat of rape is often the hub around which knightly action rotates in medieval romances."[65] Vines notes that the "aggression takes place outside of the main plot of the story" and "provide the opportunity for the heroes of these romances, such as Lancelot, Yvain, and even Arthur himself, to augment their own chivalric reputations."[66] Though the tales sometimes feature a knight's quest for atonement in order to escape punishment, the victim is often forgotten as the story moves forward toward its conclusion.

The rape motif served as a vehicle to provide an opportunity for a knight to find redemption and prove his chivalric worth. The rape itself, as Vines indicated, rarely served as the focal point of the story. Incest, however, often served as the primary complication of the narratives. Relationships of incest, both of affinity and consanguinity, occurred or almost took place in several of the tales. Some stories featured potential incest narrowly averted due to sudden recognition by the parties involved; others depicted intentional acts and yet another incest by deception with the birth of a central

---

[65] Vines 161

figure resulting from incestual sex.

The Arthurian romance *Cligés* contained incest based on a violation of affinity regulations. Alexander, emperor of Greece and Constantinople, fathers two sons, Alexander and Alis. The son Alexander, as the eldest, stands to inherit his father's wealth and become emperor upon his father's death. Though Alexander is the rightful heir to the throne, the younger Alis assumes power when Alexander travels to England to fight as a knight under King Arthur. While in England Alexander falls in love with and marries King Arthur's niece, Soredamors. Soon after a boy, Cligés, is born.

When Alexander learns that Alis has usurped the throne after the death of their father he travels to Greece to confront his brother. The siblings reach an agreement whereby Alis can retain the title of emperor but Cligés will ascend to the throne upon the death of his brother. In order to facilitate the arrangement Alis agrees that he will never marry and have children which would leave Cligés as the rightful heir to the throne. Sometime later, after the death of his brother Alexander, a marriage is

---

[66] Vines 162

arranged between Alis and Fernice, the daughter of a German emperor. Though the marriage takes place for political reasons it still violates the agreement between the siblings.

A complication ensues when, prior to the wedding, Cligés meets Fernice and falls in love with her and she with him. Neither acknowledges the attraction for the other at first. Fernice does not wish to marry Alis but feels compelled to do so and when she does she becomes Cligés' aunt. In an effort to avoid having sexual intercourse with Alis, Fernice enlists the aid of her nurse Thessala who concocts a potion that causes Alis to dream that he had sex with his wife though they never actually did. Eventually Cligés and Fernice admit their feelings for one another and create a plan to run off together. Fernice makes a statement to Cligés that "your uncle never had a part of me...He has never yet known me as Adam knew his wife."[67] Perhaps this indicated that the union would not constitute incest since the marriage was never consummated, though the marriage existed in the eyes of the law.

---

[67] Cligés 187

Alis later dies leaving Fernice and Cligés free to marry. This represented a violation of consanguinity protocols since affinity regulations prohibit a person from marrying their in-laws even though there is no blood relation between Cligés and Fernice. The argument in their favor stems from the fact that the union was not consummated, though without an annulment of the marriage of Fernice and Alis it appears incestuous in terms of Church protocols.

The significant element in the story is one of identity. Are Fernice and Cligés, in fact, related? Fernice did marry the uncle of Cligés but the marriage was never consummated. Leslie Dunton-Downer explores the issue in her essay, "The Horror of Culture: East West Incest in Chrétien de Troyes's Cligés" and postulates that the issue of incest serves as the framework for the story:

> The double functioning of the incest
> problem (that is, who is inside and who is
> outside "the family") is textually
> reproduced in several different ways,
> with the question of cultural origins and

authority framing the entire

composition.[68]

The concept of man and woman becoming "one flesh"

after intercourse suggest that the pair is not related since

there was no consummation of the marriage and as such,

"The innocence of the lovers Fernice and Cligés is

therefore technically intact."[69] In a legal sense Cligés and

Fernice became brother and sister-in-law once Fernice

and Alis wed. Regardless, this issue concerns affinity

rather than consanguinity as there is no blood

relationship between the two. Perhaps Chrétien wrote

the story in response to the questions or concerns of his

audience about what constitutes an incestuous

relationship.

Reflecting this confusion, Fernice found herself

conflicted by her desire for Cligés and expressed her

concern to her nurse:

...the emperor is marrying me, which

makes me sad and angry, for the one I

love is the nephew of the man I must wed.

And if the emperor takes his pleasure of

---

[68] Dunton-Downer 373

me, then I will have lost my own

happiness and can expect no other.[70]

Fernice's lament suggests that she believes that if the marriage isn't consummated she will be free to love Cligés. There exists another possibility however, she could be concerned with a loss of virginity and being something less than a pure woman rather than becoming related to Cligés by affinity.

The final tale of Chrétien's Arthurian romances, "The Story of the Grail," serves as an example of incest averted. The knight Gawain becomes the central character in the latter part of the story. Gawain sees a castle and asks a boatman about it. The boatman tells him that "there is a queen, a lady who is very noble, rich and wise, and of the highest lineage." The woman lives there with another lady "she calls her queen and daughter, and this second lady herself has a daughter." The boatman also tells Gawain that "the hall is very well protected by magic and enchantment."[71] In addition there are a great many people living in the castle waiting

---

[69] Dunton-Downer 370
[70] Chrétien 161
[71] Chrétien 473

for something the boatman calls "an absurd impossible event" to happen which is for a savior to arrive and lift the spell :

> ...they are waiting for a knight who'll
> come there to protect them, to restore
> their inheritances to the ladies, to give
> husbands to the maidens, and to make the
> squires knights....he [the knight] would
> have to be perfectly wise and generous,
> lacking all covetousness, fair and noble,
> bold and loyal, with no trace of
> wickedness or evil. If such a knight were
> to come there, he could rule the hall and
> return their lands...and in quick
> succession rid the hall of its magic spells.[72]

Happy to hear this, Gawain proceeded to the fortress. He entered the castle and enchantments appeared in the form of arrows directed at him. Gawain survived the arrows but was attacked by a lion, which he killed. This ended the enchantment and lifted the spell. He was hailed as a hero and told "you are the one we have long

---

[72] Chrétien 474

been awaiting."[73]

Gawain encountered Guiromelant who informed him that the queen of the castle was the mother he hadn't seen in twenty years. Two decades earlier his mother came to the castle "heavy with child" which was the sister Gawain had never met. The other queen would then be his grandmother. Later in the hall for "merry-making" Gawain sat beside his sister who did not yet know who he was as she said, "Alas, my brother doesn't even know I was born, and has never seen me!"[74] As the siblings were speaking the two queens, Gawain's mother and grandmother, watched with the older queen saying:

> 'Good daughter, what do you think of this
> lord who is sitting beside your daughter,
> my granddaughter? He's been whispering
> to her for a long time...it's a sign of his
> great nobility that he's attracted to the
> most beautiful and wisest woman in the
> hall...May it please God that he marry
> her.'[75]

---

[73] Chrétien 477
[74] Chrétien 491
[75] Chrétien 491

With the younger queen's response Chrétien injects a bit of humor. Though the women are not yet aware of the relationship, the readers certainly are. The younger queen says, "may God grant him to love her as a brother loves a sister, and may he so love her and she him that the two become one flesh."[76] The concept of "one flesh" originates in the Bible as the sexual joining of two people which contradicts the notion of loving each other as brother and sister, this points directly to the theme of incest.

Chrétien did not finish the story so a final resolution never occurred. Since the sister became aware of her relationship to Gawain the assumption of the grandmothers being informed of the relationship seems plausible. No certainty exists that incest would have happened if recognition hadn't occurred but the tale still serves as an example of the motif of incest averted through recognition.

The incest story familiar to many, between Arthur and Morgause, the wife of King Lot, did not become part of the Arthurian lore until the Thirteenth

---

[76] Chrétien 491

Century, a relatively late addition. In some versions of the tales Morgan le Fay rather than Morgause commits the incestuous act with her half-brother Arthur. Thomas Malory described the encounter with Margause as the central character in his work, *Le Morte Darthur*, and did so with little fanfare as if it were not a significant event:

> ...she came richly beseen, with her four
> sons Gawain, Gaheris, Agravian, and
> Gareth, with many other knights and
> ladies, for she was a passing fair lady.
> Wherefore the King cast great love unto
> her, and desired to lie by her. And so they
> were agreed, and he begot upon her Sir
> Mordred, and she was sister on the
> mother's side, Igraine, unto Arthur.[77]

Arthur had no awareness of the consanguineous relationship, "King Arthur knew not King Lot's wife was his sister,"[78] but he did know she of her marriage and therefore the liaison constituted adultery.

Archibald commented of the relatively benign nature of Malory's depiction of the encounter:

---

[77] Malory 21

When the story of his encounter first
appeared, moral comment is curiously
lacking. It could have been the ultimate
cautionary tale – but Arthurian writers
seem to have shied away from making
much of it.[79]

For a man of Arthur's prominence and seeming high
moral fiber, this encounter shows a different, more
human side in that he gave in to lust and committed
adultery with the wife of another king and, though
inadvertently, committed an incestuous act with his half-
sister. While Arthur maintained a degree of innocence
because he was unaware he was committing an act of
incest, but that innocence dissipates because he
knowingly engaged in an act of adultery. The drastic
consequences that ensued would seem to suggest that a
more robust description of the event would have been
appropriate.

The coupling led to the birth of Arthur's son
Mordred. Unlike other children of incest, such as Hrolf
Kraki, Mordred did not become a heroic figure; instead

---

[78] Malory 21

he would become the instrument of Arthur's destruction. Merlin informs Arthur of what he has inadvertently done and the consequences of the act:

> But ye have done a thing late that God is displeased with you, for ye have lain by your sister, and on her ye have begotten a child that shall destroy you and all the knights of your realm...for it is God's will that your body should be punished for your foul deeds.[80]

In an attempt to alter the prophesy Arthur makes another morally questionable decision. Merlin informed Arthur that the child was born on May Day. The king does not know who the child is so Arthur orders that all children born on that day are to report to him:

> Wherefore he sent for them all, on pain of death; and so there were found many lords' sons and many knights' sons, and were all sent unto the King. And so was Mordred sent by King Lot's wife; and all were put in a ship to the sea, and some

---

[79] Archibald 203

> were four weeks old, and some less. And
> so by fortune the ship drove unto a castle
> and was all to-riven, and destroyed the
> most part save that Mordred was cast
> up;[81]

In his effort to counter Merlin's prophesy Arthur
caused the death of many innocent children yet Mordred
survived. The mass infanticide shows a different Arthur,
rather than a benevolent ruler he becomes a ruthless
king willing to sacrifice others in his quest for self-
preservation which, along with the adulterous and
incestuous coupling with Lot's wife, is indicative of a
moral decay in Arthur's realm.

In the earlier versions of the tale Modred is not
Arthur's son but, rather, his nephew. Geoffrey of
Monmouth history told of Mordred and Guinevere's
affair while Arthur was away in Rome:

> ...news reached Arthur that his nephew
> Mordred, in whose keeping he had left
> the governance of Britain, had proven
> himself to be a tyrant and a traitor.

---

[80] Malory 23

> Mordred had seized the throne of Britain
> and now took his wicked pleasure with
> Guinevere, who had broken her marriage
> vows.[82]

This version not only constitutes adultery, it is incest by affinity since Mordred, in this case, is Arthur's nephew and, by the doctrine of one-flesh, related to Guinevere. Geoffrey, however, provides no indication of such a union being incestuous in his account though it certainly violates Church protocols.

Malory's much later version casts Mordred as Arthur's illegitimate and incestuous son but depicts a different outcome in regard to Guinevere. Mordred falsified letters proclaiming that Arthur and Lancelot had been killed in battle and called upon the lords to proclaim him king of England.

> And afterward he drew him unto
> Winchester, and there he took Queen
> Guinevere and said plainly that he would
> wed her, which was his uncle's wife and
> his father's wife. And so he made ready

---

[81] Mallory 31

for the feast, and a day prefixed that they
should be wedded, wherefore Queen
Guinevere was passing heavy; but she
durst not discover her heart, but she
spoke and agreed to Sir Mordred's will.[83]

Malory leaves no doubt as to incest with his reference to
"his uncle's wife and his father's wife." The difference
stems from the lack of consummation of the marriage. By
telling Mordred that she needed to prepare for the
wedding and purchase needed items, Guinevere instead
fled to the Tower of London in order to escape him and
"that she had liever slay herself than to be married to
him."[84]

Both Geoffrey's and Malory's version contain the
element of incest. In Geoffrey, though not explicitly
stated, meets the definition of incest by affinity. Malory's
tale shows the common motif of incest, in this case of
consanguinity, narrowly averted by the intended victim
fleeing from her oppressor.

---

[82] Geoffrey 196
[83] Malory 505
[84] Malory 507

The use of incest as an exemplary tale requires that those committing the sin suffer the consequences of their actions. The Arthurian tales contain two perpetrators of incest, Arthur inadvertently and Mordred intentionally. Arthur compounds his sin with his attempt to destroy the fruit of his incestuous union thereby eliminating the possibility of absolution due to ignorance. That Arthur's sin occurred without intent but Modred acted deliberately casts the latter as the villain. Modred's punishment derives from his sinful intention regardless of whether the act reached his desired conclusion. Fittingly each of them served as the instrument of the other's demise.

Much speculation exists as to the reason for the late addition of incest to the legend. Fanni Bogdanow believes that "Mordred's incestuous birth seems to serve mainly to heighten the horror of the final tragedy."[85] In her essay, "Legal Archetypes in the Arthurian Legends: the Theme of Incest,"Anca Magiru speculates that "the incestuous relationship between Arthur and Morgan-le-Fay (Morgause) is suggestive of the moral and social

---

[85] Bogdanow 143

decay of Arthur's kingdom."[86] Archibald states that "it is certain that moralizing incest stories were in vogue in the twelfth and thirteenth centuries."[87] Perhaps the incest supplies a rationale for the ultimate destruction of Arthur's realm and provides a final dramatic element that allows the legend of Camelot to come to a close. In terms of the late insertion of the incest motif Archibald writes:

> There can be no conclusive answer to the question of why the incest story was inserted into the Arthurian legend. The writer(s) may have wanted to make Arthur commit a sexual sin which would provide a moral explanation for the collapse of his world.[88]

There is no reasoning as to why the legend needed to end. The tales had circulated for centuries and the reading public's appetite for the stories seemed intact.

Incest did change the view of King Arthur from a seemingly perfect and indestructible hero to a man with

[86] Magiru 1112
[87] Archibald 218
[88] Archibald 217

very human failings. Rather than a knight and king of the highest moral fiber, Arthur now exists as a sinner committing adultery and incest – the fatal flaw that leads to his death and destruction as a tragic hero.

Richard J. Warren

Chapter 6
Chaucer & Gower

Sexual themes appeared in the late Fourteenth Century writing of Geoffrey Chaucer and his contemporary, John Gower. The fact that Chaucer wrote in English contributed to the popularity of the *Canterbury Tales* as did their content. The humor found in the stories and ribald nature of many tales resonated with those reading or hearing the words. The frame narrative of the *Canterbury Tales* allowed Chaucer to cover many topics and often wrote of adultery and rape but only obliquely approached incest with just one overt reference and several allusions to incestuous relationships found in mythological stories such as that of *Apollonius of Tyre*. Gower took a much more direct approach to the subject.

The theme of adultery served as the primary driver of Chaucer's "The Miller's Tale." John, a farmer, rents a room to a young scholar named Nicholas who falls in love with the farmer's much younger and very beautiful wife, Alisoun. Another young man, Absolon, sees the wife and immediately falls in love as well. The two young men compete for the affection of the married woman. Though Alisoun resists at first, Nicholas convinces her to have sex with him, "And spak so faire and profred hire so faste / That she hir love hym graunted atte last."[89] The humorous account of how Nicholas outwits both his rival Absolon and his lover's husband does not exhibit any sense of immorality in the actions of the lovers nor does the pair suffer any adverse consequences for their sinful behavior.

The tale that followed, "The Reeve's Tale," served to quite, or answer, the "Miller's Tale." Rather than adultery this story used the motif of rape, yet it too used humor. The story features a miller named Symkin and two young men, Aleyn and John. The miller cheats the two young men and they extract revenge by having sex with the miller's daughter and raping his wife. They felt justified because of Symkin's thievery:

[89] Chaucer 94 [ln 3289-90]

"For John," seyde he, "als" evere moot I

thryve,

If that I may, yon wenche swyve.

Some esement has lawe yshapen us,

For John, ther is a lawe that says thus:

That gif a man in a point be ygreved.

That in another he sal be releved,

Oure corn is stoln. Shortly is ne nay,

And we han had il fit al this day.

And Syn I sal have been amendedement

Agayn my los, I wil have esement.

By God[es] sa[u]le, it sal neen other bee!"[90]

The daughter willingly acquiesced to sex but the wife
believed her husband climbed on her and remained
unaware of the fact that John raped her. Not only did
Chaucer illustrate the sin of rape, he provided the
justification for it by stating the boys deserved
compensation for their loss.

The "Miller's Tale" and the "Reeve's Tale"
certainly featured sexual themes as well as the sins of
adultery and rape, but in the "Parson's Tale" Chaucer

---

[90] Chaucer 108 ln 4177-87

communicated his thoughts regarding incest when the Parson enumerated various sins including those of the flesh:

> The fourthe spece is the assemblee of hem that been of hire kynrede or of hem that been of oon affynytee or elles wih hem with whiche hir fadres or hir kynrede han deled in the synne of lecherie. This synne maketh hem lyk to houndes that taken no kepe to kynrede.
>
> And certes, parentele is in twop maneres – pouther ghostly or flesshly. Goostly as for to deelen with his godsibbes. For right so as he that engendreth a child is his flesshly fader, right so is his godfader espiritueel, for which a womman may in so lasse sinne assemblee with hire godsib than with hire owene flesshy brother.[91]

In keeping with Church protocols, the Parson makes no distinction between relationship by blood or through kinship created as a result of marriage. Archibald points

---

[91] Chaucer 443

out that "he too emphasizes spiritual incest, commenting that it is as sinful to sleep with her 'godsib' (child of her godparent or parent of her godchild) as with her own brother."[92]

While Chaucer alludes to many well-known stories of incest from mythology, "The Man of Law's Tale" contains the only direct reference to an incestuous relationship in any of the *Canterbury Tales*:

> But certeinly no word ne writeth he
> Of thilke wikke ensample of Canacee,
> That loved hir owene brother synfully --
> Of swiche cursed stories I sey fy! --
> Or ellis of Tyro Appollonius,
> How that the cursed kyng Antiochus
> Birafte his doghter of hir maydenhede,
> Whan he hir threw upon the pavement.
> And therfore he, of ful avysement,
> Nolde nevere write in none of his
> sermons
> Of swiche unkynde abhomynacions,
> Ne I wol noon reherce, if that I may.

[But certainly no word writes he

Of that wicked example of Canace,

Who loved her own brother sinfully --

Of such cursed stories I say fie! --

Or else of Apollonius of Tyre,

How that the cursed king Antiochus

Deprived his daughter of her

maidenhead,

When he threw her upon the pavement.

And therefore he, after careful

consideration

Would never write in any of his

compositions

Of such unnatural abominations,

Nor will I tell any such, if that I may.] [ln

77-89][93]

The story of Canace as told by Ovid in *Heroides* first appears in Greek mythology. She conceives a child by her brother Macareus and later commits suicide after the incestuous liaison comes to the attention of her father. The "he" referenced in the passage, "he, after careful

---

[93] Chaucer 116

consideration / Would never write in any of his compositions /Of such unnatural abominations," is Chaucer. While he showed little reservation in regards to depicting adultery, rape or abuse, he clearly stated he would not offer tales of relationships that violated the bounds of consanguinity or what he considered natural affinity. Many see this statement as a rebuke of his contemporary, John Gower. C. David Benson writes, "Scholars since at least as early as Tyrwhitt, while puzzling over Chaucer's exact motive, have generally agreed that the Man of Law's comments here are a jibe at Gower's *Confessio Amantis*" and Gower's willingness to address subjects Chaucer will not.[94]

Gower showed little of Chaucer's hesitation in discussing incest. The account of Canace and a version of *Apollonius of Tyre* appear in Gower's *Confessio Amantis*. Book three of *Confessio*, titled "Wrath" tells the tale of Canace and her brother Macareus, a story from Greek mythology. The brother-sister relationship from childhood evolved into something more in adulthood:

Sister and brother shared the same

---

[94] Benson 100

Apartment, night as well as day,

When they were young, and there would
play

Together as all children do.

And this continued while they grew

To that fresh spring of lustiness

When nature first begins to oppress

The heart with love, and makes it yield

Till Reason's laws are all repealed

And hers have sole authority.[95]

Gower shows lust as a force of nature and more
powerful than reason. Macareus "with all his heart and
soul, / Beheld her as through lover's eyes."[96] The illicit
coupling resulted in pregnancy for Canace, an obvious
consequence of their sin.

The *Apollonius of Tyre* story found in book eight
of *Confessio*, according to Archhibald, "was extremely
popular throughout the Middle Ages and into the
Renaissance, though the reasons for this popularity are
hard to pin down."[97] Perhaps the illicit nature proved

---

[95] Gower [Tiller] 127
[96] Gower [Tiller] 128
[97] Archibald 95

titillating to readers or personal experiences aroused interest in the tales. Other factors involving simple curiosity or ignorance of the boundaries of affinity relationships remain possibilities for such interest.

Early in book eight of his *Confessio Amantis* Gower outlines the Church's consanguinity protocols for marriage:

> Confessor:
>
> But though the Pope forbids us, in
>
> His Canon Law, to wed our kin
>
> Within the second or third –Though it is
>
> Holy Church's word
>
> That bounds our unions with degrees –
>
> It is not seldom one sees
>
> The rage of lechery, today
>
> Take what it will, and where it may.[98]

Through the words of the confessor, Gower makes a clear statement that despite Church prohibitions incest occurs with a degree of frequency. Referring to it as a "rage of lechery" and also as a "voluptuous desire" which

---

[98] Gower [Tiller] 260

"spares not a thought for kin,"[99] indicates that incestuous lust contains more power than any Church law.

Gower takes on his own persona in response to the priest-confessor and replies that "Never am I so wild a man / That nearest kin, and dearest, can / Inspire that sort of love in me."[100] Gower portrays himself a better man for rising above physical lust of one's relatives. Archibald states that "Gower makes the story the last in his long series of cautionary tales about love."[101] Additionally Archibald extends credit to Gower for the proliferation of incest narratives in medieval literature:

> The opening incest episode seems to be at least partly responsible for the popularity of the Apollonius story throughout the Middle Ages. Some writers felt it necessary to apologize for it, but they also emphasized that however sordid the story, it did show vice punished and virtue rewarded.[102]

---

[99] Gower [Tiller] 260
[100] Gower [Tiller] 261
[101] Archibald 100
[102] Archibald 101

Therein lay the purpose of the story – to serve as a cautionary tale to those tempted to engage in an incestuous relationship. The popularity may well derive from the hidden desires, or at least curiosities, of the tale's audience.

Sebastian Sobecki suggests another purpose for including the Apollonius story. Rather than an exemplar to the general population, it served as a cautionary tale to King Richard II, the king who commissioned Gower to write *Confessio Amantis*. Sobecki stated, "I will argue that Gower's tale of 'Apollonius of Tyre' ...offers a lesson on the paramount value of political consent and baronial advice, a lesson delivered during the turbulent years of the King's coming of age" and done "for the benefit of reforming Richard."[103] Sobecki explains the rationale for his argument:

> Gower's treatment of the incest motif is
> embedded into his discussion of kingship,
> which, like incest, emerges as being
> subject to legal discourses. The antidote to
> bad kingship and incest is administered in

---

[103] Sobecki 206

the form of good governance and
marriage, two concepts that were
undergoing radical reform at the time,
namely the introduction of consent as
their foundation. I will argue, therefore,
that the successful integration of political
and marital consent as a condition for
good rule lies at the heart of Gower's
advice to the inexperienced monarch.[104]
Sobecki acknowledges that "readers disagree in whether
the last book of the *Confessio*...conveys political advice or
instruction in any form."[105] The discussion matters little
in terms of the tale's popularity. Many, if not most
readers, likely had little inkling that the tale served to
educate or advise the king.

Before recounting the Apollonius story Gower's
work told of Caligula engaging in sexual activity with
his three sisters and taking their virginity:

An emperour was for to blame,

Gayus Caligula be name,

Which of his own sostres thre

---

[104] Sobecki 206

6789789898

Berefte the virginté:[106]

This tale served as a cautionary note in that God punished Caligula, "God hath beraft him in his ire / His lif and ek his large empire."[107] The loss of both life and empire indicate the seriousness of the offense. Gower also told of Amon's incestuous liaison with his sister and Lot's seduction by his own daughters.

Apollonius of Tyre tells of King Antiochus. His wife, the queen, died and the king could not resist his sexual desire for his own daughter:

The king, which made mochel mone[108]

Tho stod, as who seith, al him one

Withoute wif, but natheles

His doghter, which was piereles

Of beauté, duelte about him stille.

Bot whanne a man hath welthe at wille,

The fleissh is frele and falleth ofte

And that this maide tendre and softe

Which in hire fadres and chambers duelte,

Withinne a time wiste and felte.

[105] Sobecki 207-08

[106] Gower 199

[107] Gower 199

For likinge and concupiscence[109]

Withoute insihte of conscience

The fader so with lustes blente,

That he caste al his hole entente

His oghne doghter for to spille.[110]

The king proved powerless over his own lust and slept
with his daughter. The rest of the tale involves
Apollonius and his family but Antiochus figures
prominently. Apollonius approaches the king as a suitor
to his daughter. Antiochus tells him he must solve a
riddle if he wishes permission to woo his daughter:

With felonie I am upbore

I ete and have it not forbore

Mi moderes fleissh, who housebonde

Mi fader for to seche I fonde,

Which is the sone ek my wif.

Apollonius solves the riddle which, much like the Exeter
Book riddle of Lot, reveals the incestuous relationship of
the king and his daughter. This places Apollonius in
great danger and much of the story concerns his

---

[108] alone by himself
[109] carnal lust
[110] Gower 202

adventures as he seeks to survive. Salvation arrives in the form of a lightning bolt which strikes Antiochus and his daughter dead. The death blow from the heavens warns of God's retribution for those who succumb to the sin of incest.

Unlike the conservative Chaucer, Gower makes no attempt to camouflage incest or merely hint about its occurrence. Additional elements could account for Gower's willingness to test the boundaries of depicting social taboos. In his book, *Gower's Vulgar Tongue*, T. Matthew N. McCabe postulates that Gower sensed a shift in appetites of his readership due to an increasing desire for upward social mobility:

> The late medieval proliferation of conduct
> books and other trappings of aristocratic
> culture among the lower gentry and
> middle estates attests the extent to which
> socially ambitious readers from the
> merchant, civil servant, small
> landowning, and other middle groups
> found these materials useful as a means to

upward mobility.[111]

Many narratives frequently feature kings or other high nobility as the perpetrators of incestuous acts. Public resistance to strict consanguinity protocols seem a more likely reason for people to desire for stories featuring this motif than seeing them as tool for upward mobility. The illustration of the vulnerability of the elite to sins of the flesh show that those of the highest status are not without flaws.

Whatever the motivation of the audience, Chaucer and Gower approach their readership differently. Chaucer not only shows a distaste for incestuous tales, he makes a point of saying he won't demean himself to do so ("But certainly no word writes he"). The statement that such tales are too horrible to tell informs his readers that to engage in such activity represents an egregious offense.

Rather than tell his readers such tales are too sinful to repeat, Gower uses his reader's desire for the stories to provide his message. In *The Chaucer Review* Benson states that, "The *Confessio Amantis* is a work

---

[111] McCabe 5

about love, and Gower is educating his readers in the dangers of excessive, non-rational passion."[112] Benson suggests that Gower sees sexual impulse in humans as dictated by nature but controllable through the use of superior intellect and high moral standards:

> Gower follows orthodox medieval
> thought in pro claiming that while
> mankind shares a common "kynde" with
> all other animals, he alone has another,
> higher nature as a result of his reason. To
> obey only the dictates of his lower nature,
> such as the sexual impulse, is thus to
> reduce himself to the level of a mere beast
> and deny his humanity. [113]

The characters in Gower's stories suffer consequences for their actions. Canace's guilt over her sin drives her to suicide. Antiochus and his daughter are felled by a lightning bolt as punishment for their incestuous relationship. The message resonates clearly; sinners will suffer the wrath of God for violating the protocols on

---

[112] Benson 105

[113] Benson 102-03

consanguinity. Chaucer delivers his message subtly and Gower in a much more overt manner but both demonstrated that incest represents a violation of the laws of man, nature, and God.

Chapter 7
Renaissance Drama

As England moved from the late Middle Ages
into the Renaissance language and literature evolved.
The Great Vowel Shift transformed Middle English into
the Early Modern variety. William Caxton's introduction
of the printing press moved the writing process away
from monastic scribes and toward commercial printers
with stories such as Chaucer's *Canterbury Tales* increasing
in popularity with the public. The focus of literature
changed along with it as the medieval emphasis on
Christianity and the soul, as well as chivalry, turned to a
revival of the classics and man in general. Throughout
the climatic shift in the hub of literary attention one
constant remained – the reading public's fascination with
the incest motif, as seen in works such as Christopher
Marlowe's *Hero and Leander* with "Jove slyly stealing

from his sister's bed."[114] This allure shows itself most
clearly in Renaissance drama and the works of John Ford
and William Shakespeare.

Ford's drama, *'Tis Pity She's a Whore*, centers
around Giovanni's desire for his sister Annabella. Ford
makes no attempt to disguise the incest but rather
introduces it in the first scene of Act I when Giovanni
discusses his illicit desire with a friar who attempts to
dissuade him from committing a sin. Giovanni pleads,
"Must I not do what all men else may – love?"[115] The friar
assures him that he may seek romance, but when
Giovanni wishes to love his own sister the friar calls him
a "foolish madman."[116] Not satisfied with the friar's
response, Giovanni continues to plead his case:

> Shall a peevish sound,
>
> A customary form, from man to man,
>
> Of brother and a sister, be a bar
>
> 'Twixt my perpetual happiness and me?[117]

Introducing the theme of incest at the outset of the
drama represents a change of style from the medieval

---

[114] Marlowe
[115] Ford ln.18
[116] Ford ln. 24

era in that the plot centers upon the taboo rather than showing it as a causative agent of some complication. Ford introduces the Church doctrine of "one flesh" a few lines later when Giovanni states, "...to be ever one, / One soul, one flesh, one love, one heart, one all?"[118] After the friar tells him that he is a lost soul Giovanni continues his lament stating, "Shall then, for that I am her brother born, / My joys be ever banished from her bed?"[119] He then asks the friar for a solution:

> Giovanni: Tell me holy man,
>
> What cure shall give me ease in these
>
> extremes?
>
> Friar: Repentance son, and sorrow for this
>
> sin;
>
> For though hast moved a Majesty above
>
> With thy unranged almost blasphemy[120]

The friar's call for repentance reflects the attitude of prior ages so the concept of incest as a grave sin remains unchanged.

---

[117] Ford ln. 25-28
[118] Ford ln. 33-34
[119] Ford ln. 36-37
[120] Ford ln. 42-45

Unlike many stories where incest is averted in some manner, Annabella learns of Giovanni's desire for her and willingly consummates the relationship. As a consequence she becomes pregnant and marries another suitor because she cannot wed her own brother. Her new husband learns of her pregnancy and it soon becomes known that the father is her own brother Giovanni. In the fashion of a tragedy this complication creates a series of calamitous events that leave the majority of the characters dead. Renaissance depictions of incest vary from the earlier forms of medieval literature in that rather than the perpetrators of incest suffering the consequences of their sin, those around them are brought down along with them. Archibald makes note of this as well:

> In Renaissance drama the incestuous
> protagonists tend to drag everyone else
> down with them....There can be no
> recovery from consummated incest in
> these plays; villains and victims alike
> must die.[121]

---

[121] Archibald 236

Whereas earlier writers simply focused on incest being an evil sin, Renaissance authors explored the motivations behind the act as Richard McCabe points out in *Incest, Drama, and Nature's Law*:

> The incestuous and all they represent are effectively abandoned to a deterministic psychosis that may be termed "sin" only is the sense that...the absence of grace is sin. The most challenging plays...confront the stark truth that aberration is integral to human nature.[122]

The view of incest, rather than a personal tragedy of the sinner's soul, now belongs to society as a whole. Rather than consequences suffered by an individual, all involved, even peripherally share in the fate.

Shakespeare embraced the incest motif in several of his plays, sometimes obliquely but often overtly. Some view King Lear's fixation on his youngest daughter, Cordelia, as incestuous desire. Elizabeth Boyce states that "the motif of incest in King Lear is subtle, but it is the basis on which the entire tragic plot unfolds."

---

[122] McCabe 294

Though the dialogue exhibits no blatantly sexual banter between Lear and Odelia, Boyce suggests the existence of "one of Shakespeare's most complicated father-daughter relationships." [123] Lear's love for Odelia obviously shows but the more suggestive dialogue occurs between the king and his two other daughters, Goneril and Regan. Goneril states she loves her father, "As much as child e'er loved, or father found. / A love that makes breath poor, and speech unable – / Beyond all manner of so much I love you."[124] Regan stated that, "I profess myself an enemy to all other joys."[125] Odelia called her sister's relationships with their father inappropriate when she stated, "Why have my sisters husbands, if they say / They love you all?"[126] That Odelia did not love him the way his other daughters had displeased Lear so much that he banished her and disinherited her. Though no clear representation of sexual contact occurs between Lear and any of his daughters, a closer bond than a traditional father-

---

[123] Boyce par. 11
[124] Lear 1.1 61-63
[125] Lear 1.1 75

[126] Lear 1.1 101-02

daughter relationship seems present allowing for speculation of an existence of incestuous desire, if not intent.

In *Pericles, Prince of Tyre* Shakespeare retells the story of *Apollonius of Tyre* which Chaucer alluded to and Gower told in his *Confessio Amantis*. Shakespeare's play even includes Gower as a character introduced in the opening scene, "To sing a song that old was sung / From ashes ancient Gower has come."[127] Boyce states that the play "contains the most overt and terrifying portrayal of incest in Shakespeare's canon."[128] Indeed, no attempt to camouflage incest occurs at all as the opening lines make clear:

> This king unto him took a fere,[129]
>
> Who died and left a female heir
>
> So buxom, blithe and full of face
>
> As heaven had lent her all his grace
>
> With whom the father liking took
>
> And her to incest did provoke.[130]

---

[127] Pericles 1.1 ln 1-2
[128] Boyce par. 2
[129] Companion
[130] Pericles 1.1 ln 21-26

As in Gower's story, suitors must solve a riddle to gain permission from King Antiochus to woo his daughter. In Shakespeare's version Pericles assumes the role of Apollonius and must solve the riddle:

> I am no viper, yet I feed
> On mother's flesh which did me breed.
> I sought a husband, in which labour
> I found that kingdom in a father.
> He's father, son, and husband mild;
> I mother, wife, and yet his child.
> How they may be, and yet in two,
> As you will live resolve it you.[131]

From this point the story moves in a similar fashion to Gower's *Apollonius*. Pericles flees Antioch and later fathers a child he believes died in a shipwreck. They meet fourteen years later but before anything sexual occurs they realize their father-daughter relationship which serves as an example of incest averted by recognition.

Shakespeare's *Pericles* retold the story Gower acquired from Latin or Greek sources showing that the

---

[131] Pericles 1.1 ln 65-72

incest motif survived from antiquity without losing appeal. Boyce speculates on the reason for the popularity:

> Incest remains the top of taboos and all societies show what Freud called 'Insestcheu,' avoidance of incest. However these plays expose a disturbing reality that, despite our abhorrence of it, human nature does not truly have an aversion to incest.[132]

Shakespeare certainly embraced the public's fascination with the incest motif. Though *Pericles* exhibits the most obvious reference to the topic, a play written almost a decade earlier gathers the most discussion of the taboo.

Shakespeare's *Hamlet* centers on incest, but not the variety of mother-son that many with a Freudian view seem to believe. McCabe states that "*Hamlet* is equally rooted in the soil of the incest complex, but under a better disguise."[133] So while Hamlet's jealousy of Gertrude's marriage to Claudius permeates the play, no scene shows any consummation of incest between

---

[132] Boyce par. 2

mother and son. There are, however, a number of references to incest of affinity. Leviticus 18 states, "'Do not have sexual relations with your brother's wife; that would dishonor your brother."[134] When Gertrude marries her brother-in-law Claudius it represents incest in that constitutes a violation of the doctrine of "one flesh." Hamlet remarks on the speed with which his mother remarried, "But not two months dead," and on her weakness, "Frailty, thy name is woman." He goes on to state his displeasure with the union of his mother and uncle:

> ...married with my uncle
>
> My father's brother, but no more like my
>
> father
>
> Than I to Hercules. Within a month
>
> Ere yet the salt of most unrighteous tears
>
> Had left flushing in her galled eyes
>
> She married. O most wicked speed, to
>
> post

---

[133] McCabe 6
[134] Levitcus 18.16

> With such dexterity to incestuous
>
> sheets.[135]

Hamlet seems more upset by the speed with which Gertrude moved on after his father's death but he does refer to the marriage as incestuous. Later in the play Hamlet refers to Claudius as his mother:

> Hamlet: Farewell dear mother.
>
> Claudius: Thy loving father, Hamlet.
>
> Hamlet: My mother. Father and mother is
>
> man and wife, man and wife is one flesh
>
> and so my mother.[136]

In his essay, "Aspects of the Incest Problem in *Hamlet*," Jason Rosenbatt comments on this exchange and states, "Aside from carrying the logic of incest to its conclusion by fusing Claudius, Gertrude, and his dead father, Hamlet reminds the King of the very basis of affinity."[137] Hamlet references the affinity violation numerous times. He calls Claudius his "uncle-father" and Gertrude as his "aunt-mother." [138] He refers again to Claudius "in the

---

[135] Hamlet 1.2 ln 151-57
[136] Hamlet 4.3 ln 50-53
[137] Rosenblatt 350
[138] Hamlet 2.2

incestuous pleasure of his bed" with Gertrude.[139] He
speaks to Gertrude of her marriage, "Mother you have
my father much offended" and reminds her of her sin,
"You are the Queen, your husband's brother's wife /
And would it were not so you are my mother."[140] The
statement suggests Hamlet wishes he'd never been born
as Rosneblatt says:

> It is difficult to refrain from developing
> the point that existence is indeed
> problematic for Hamlet – that he feels
> tainted, even before the Ghost has
> appeared to him, because Gertrude's
> incestuous guilt is somehow involved
> with his birth.[141]

McCabe traces the incest to the play's opening scene
suggesting that the beginning foreshadowed the final
tragedy:

> Were one to read the acts and scenes of
> *Hamlet* in reverse order, attempting to
> trace the hero's tragic malady to its root,

---

[139] Hamlet 3.3 ln 90
[140] Hamlet 3.4 ln 14-15
[141] Rosenblatt 363

the investigation would proceed past the
Ghost and the first soliloquy to the single
line which serves to introduce us to the
consciousness of the prince: "a little more
than kin, and less than kind." (1.2.65)[142]

Claudius added step-father to his role as Hamlet's uncle,
thus more than kin. Hamlet's darkness stems from the
taint Rosenblatt alludes to and the prince's resentment of
his mother's relationship with his uncle. McCabe
speculates that Hamlet's comes from "his own emotional
need to evoke from within himself the profound sense of
revulsion which accusations of incest traditionally
facilitate."[143] Certainly Hamlet's turmoil results from the
emotions dredged up by the relationship and not from
any concern for violations of Church or secular
prohibitions. This suggests that incest violates the law of
nature rather than man.

As in 'Tis Pity She's a Whore and Pericles, the
consequences of incest in Hamlet result in the deaths of
most of the players. Though many factors converged to

---

[142] McCabe 162

[143] McCabe 165

create the final scene, the seeds of the tragedy were the incestuous union of Claudius and Gertrude. The shift during the Renaissance from the medieval notion of incest as a sin that harms the soul of one person to the idea of shared guilt and consequences reflects the attitudinal shift held by the population in general. Archibald states:

> Of the many important changes which took place in this period (Renaissance), two of the most influential for the incest theme were the Protestant Reformation and the new humanist interest in classical literature and culture. Classical literature was generally fatalistic; no amount of contrition could bring its protagonists grace or salvation. The Protestant Reformation was also fatalistic in a different way, in terms of an apocalyptic vision, since Protestant and Calvinistic tradition believed that the elect are predetermined.[144]

---

[144] Archibald 235

Archibald's explanation neatly accounts for differences in the consequences for those who run afoul of the incest taboo.

The Renaissance may have altered the end result of incestual sin but the appearance in literature remained frequent. Little changed in the variations found in the motif as they still contained father-daughter incest, mother-son and sibling. Incest consummated and averted occurred as did couplings due to a lack of recognition. The society of the time obviously viewed the practice as a violation of accepted mores but, like the forbidden fruit, readers and audiences still hungered for the tales as evidenced by their frequency.

Richard J. Warren

Chapter 8
Conclusion

Literary depictions of incest appear in the earliest of written works which indicates they probably evolved from oral sources. The tales from antiquity morphed into medieval stories, reappeared in Renaissance writing and survived through the years and remain with us in various forms today. Often serving a cautionary role warning of the consequences of incestual sin, the texts serve as one of the few windows to the sexual practices and attitudes of the medieval period. Surely other cautionary tales warn of the inherent evils of adultery, homosexuality and other acts thought of as sins, but many of those now lack a societal stigma. As Archibald states, "Homosexuality is no longer shocking and unmentionable in our society, incest is still shocking, and

has only recently become mentionable."[145] Among many
forms once thought of as immoral, incest remains as a
significant taboo.

That the incest taboo survived through the years
despite the presence of an increased awareness of genetic
complications and the consequences of producing
incestual offspring suggest that the fascination with the
subject is somehow ingrained within human sexuality.
The prohibition of the practice surfaces across a broad
spectrum of human society suggesting the organic, or
evolutionarily derived, rather than learned nature of the
taboo. The Darwinian process of natural selection
perhaps imbued humans with a natural aversion to
consanguineous relationships that would impact the
long-term survival of humans as a species. McCabe,
however, disagrees:

> If the taboo is indeed a product of
> evolution why does it vary so much from
> culture to culture? Incest is not unnatural
> in the same sense that mating of different
> species is unnatural; it can and does occur

---

[145] Archibald 3

and, in any case, the extrapolation of
moral laws from physical processes
constitutes an act of social
interpretation.[146]

Whatever the reason, the interest in the incest motif that
existed in the medieval period remains with us today.

Though the reason for the interest cannot be
conclusively determined, literature often provides the
only evidence of medieval sexuality and common sexual
practices in existence. As Gravdal demonstrated, though
some evidence exists in court records, official historical
documentation does not provide sufficient information
as to the nature of medieval sexuality. Manifestations of
incest and other sexual practices must be deciphered
from the literary depictions that do survive. McCabe
believes that, "it would be absurd, for example, to
postulate a simple correlation between literature and life,
[and] employing dramatic texts as sociological
documents,"[147] that literature is often the only possible
source. R.E. Gajdusek agrees with this stating, "It is in

---

[146] McCabe 21

[147] McCabe 26

the rigorous study of literary metaphors of incest that we are brought to an insight into the source of the incest taboo itself."[148]

Much of the impetus for the popularity of incest narratives came from the Church. The papal concern for eliminating the all too common sin of incest led to the creation and enforcement of consanguinity and affinity doctrines. Though rooted in Leviticus 18 and the concept of man and wife as "one flesh," Church prohibitions created a taboo in many ways similar to the forbidden fruit. The act of so strongly preaching against a practice creates a natural curiosity. That combined with the realities of medieval life and the difficulty of locating a suitable mate within the strict boundaries of the consanguinity protocols engendered a situation where the population routinely ignored the regulations out of simple necessity. Though the 4th Lateran Council of 1215 relaxed the prohibitions, the incest motif remained as a popular theme in literature.

Anglo-Saxon tales such as *Beowulf* and Norse Sagas contained various aspect of the incest theme that

---

[148] Gajdusek 158

illustrated attitudes toward the taboo in the period. Arthurian tales serve well as an example of the evolution of the incest motif as the stories appeared in both France and England and spanned the Old English, Middle English and early Modern eras. Though their popularity waned at times, the Arthurian legend highlights various forms of incest and the consequences involved. The late addition of Arthur's incest with his half-sister served a significant cautionary purpose in that the sin could destroy even the greatest of kings.

The late Fourteenth Century writing of Geoffrey Chaucer and his contemporary, John Gower demonstrated significantly different styles of dealing with the incest theme. Chaucer seemed reluctant to write about it while Gower showed little hesitation in discussing the subject. Such disparity in approach likely reflects personal attitudes of the authors to incest but may also reflect the attitudes of their readers. While Chaucer approached the subject cautiously and Gower with little fear, both authors demonstrated that incest represented a violation of the laws of nature, man, and God.

As the late Middle Ages morphed into the Renaissance bringing with it significant societal changes, the incest motif remained. The primary difference in the treatment of incest stories between the eras lay in the consequences of the sin. The theme appeared in the writings of Christopher Marlowe's *Hero and Leander* and John Ford *'Tis Pity She's a Whore* and many of Shakespeare's plays embraced the theme, Gajdusek viewed Shakespeare's usage of incest metaphorically:

> On the metaphor in the later plays of William Shakespeare, incest seems to be itself a metaphor for the dissolution of consciousness, the breakdown and yielding of the ego to the primal material from which it once emerged.[149]

This view remains consistent with the concept of the Renaissance concern with man and society in general rather than the medieval focus on the soul of an individual. The tragic consequences of incest led to the destruction of all involved rather than only the perpetrators of incest. This metaphorically indicates the

---

[149] Gajdusek 158

impact of incestual relationships on all of society rather than only the individual.

Through all the changes of literature the incest motif remains a constant. Firmly rooted in the classics with a fatalistic notion of the consequences, the incest theme moved to the Middle Ages and introduced the prospect of salvation of the sinner's soul. Curiously the revival of interest in the Classics during the Renaissance also brought about a return to the fatalistic consequences of incest as evidenced by the death of most of the players in Shakespeare's incest-centered tragedies.

The mores and expectations of society change over the course of time. Situations once thought of as taboos, such as homosexuality, mixed-race relationships, and same-sex marriage have moved into the realm of generally, though not universally, accepted practice. Incest stands as one remaining taboo that shows little indication of gaining societal acceptance. As Archibald states:

> There seems to be every reason to believe
> that the incidence of incest does not
> change much over the centuries; what

does change is the level of public

acknowledgement that it happens, and

discussion of what to do about it.[150]

Genetic consequences certainly play a role in the lack of

acceptance though the practice received widespread

disapproval prior to the discovery of a genetic link to

inbreeding. The reason for the long-standing

disapproval as well as for the inherent fascination with

the subject remains indeterminable, likely forever.

Literature does provide evidence of that inherent

fascination and allows the debate to continue, perhaps

ad infinitum.

---

[150] Archibald 7

Bibliography

Archibald, Elizabeth. "Gold in the Dungheap: Incest
    Stories and Family Values in the Middle Ages."
    Journal of Family History 22.2 (1997): 133-49. Web.

Archibald, Elizabeth. *Incest and the Medieval Imagination*.
    Oxford: Clarendon Press, 2001. Print.

Augustine, City of God Against the Pagans, trans. and
    ed. R.W. Dyson, Cambridge Texts in the History
    of Political Thought (Cambridge: Cambridge
    University Press, 2006): 665.

Baum, Paull F. 1886-1964 (Paull Franklin). *Anglo-Saxon
    Riddles of the Exeter Book*. United States: Duke
    University Press, 1963. Web.

Bede,. *Ecclesiastical History of the English People*. Trans.
    Lea Sherley-Price. London: Penguin Books, 1990.
    Print.

Bellows, Henry Adams. *The Poetic Edda: The Heroic Poems.* Trans. Mineola, New York: Dover Publications Inc, 2007. Print.

Benson, Larry D., and Edward E. Foster, eds. *King Arthur's Death: Stanzaic Morte Arthur & Alliterative Morte Arthure.* Kalamazoo: Medieval Institute Publications, 1994. Print.

Bjork, Robert E., and John D. Niles, eds. *A Beowulf Handbook.* Lincoln: University of Nebraska Press, 1977. Print.

Bogdanow, Fanni. *The Romance of the Grail: A Study of the Structure and Genesis of a Thirteenth-Century Arthurian Prose Romance.* Manchester U.P, 1966. Print.

Boyce, Elizabeth. "The Trouble of Incest in Shakespeare's Late Plays: King Lear and Pericles." *The Paper Shell Review.* University of Maryland, Spring 2015. Web. 22 Feb. 2016.

Byock, Jesse L. *The Saga of King Hrolf Kraki.* Trans. London: Penguin Books, 2007. Print.

Bullough, Vern L.; Brundage, James. Handbook of
    Medieval Sexuality. Independence: Taylor and
    Francis, 2013. Ebook Library. Web. 27 Jan. 2016.

Carroll, Robert P., Stephen Prickett, and Inc ebrary. *The
    Bible: Authorized King James Version*. Oxford
    University Press, 2008. Web.

Chaucer, Geffrey. *The Canterbury Tales*. Trans. Robert
    Boenig and Andrew Taylor. 2nd ed. Toronto:
    Broadview Press, 2012. Print.

Chrétien, . *Arthurian Romances*. London: Penguin Books,
    1991. Print.

Collins, S. A. "Sundrie Shapes, Committing Headdie
    Ryots, Incest, Rapes: Functions of Myth in
    Determining Narrative and Tone in Marlowe's
    "Hero and Leander"." *Mosaic* 4.1 (1970): 107.
    ProQuest. Web. 21 Mar. 2016.

Conlee, John W. *Prose Merlin*. Published for TEAMS in
    association with the University of Rochester by
    Medieval Institute Publications, Western
    Michigan University, 1998. Print.

Damico, Helen. *Beowulf's Wealhtheow and the Valkyrie Tradition*. Madison: The University of Wisconsin Press, 1984. Print.

Dante, . *The Divine Comedy*. Trans. Clive James. New York: Liveright Publishing, 2013. Print.

Dunton-Downer, Leslie. "The Horror of Culture: East West Incest in Chrétien De Troyes's "Cligés"". *New Literary History* 28.2 (1997): 367–381. Web.

Finch, R. G.. *The Saga of the Volsungs*. Trans. London: Thomas Nelson and Sons, Ltd., 1965. Print.

Ford, John. *'Tis Pity She's a Whore*. Manchester: Manchester University Press, 1997. Print.

Foucalt, Michel. *The History of Sexuality*. Vol. 1: An Introduction. New York: Vintage Books, 1990. Print.

"Fourth Lateran Council : 1215." *Papal Encyclicals Online* . N.p., July 2015. Web. 16 Dec. 2015.

Frantzen, Allen J. *The Anglo-Saxon Penitentials: A Cultural Database.*, 1901. Web.

Gajdusek, R. E. "Death, Incest, and the Triple Bond in the
    Later Plays of Shakespeare." *American Imago* 31.2
    (1974): 109. *ProQuest.* Web. 21 Mar. 2016.

Geoffrey of Monmouth., Michael A. Falerta, ed. *The
    History of the Kings of Britain*. Ontario: Broadview
    Editions, 2008. Print.

Gower, John. *Confessio Amantis*. Kalamazoo: Medieval
    Institute Publications, 2000. Print.

Gravdal, Kathryn. "Confessing Incests: Legal Erasures
    and Literary Celebrations in Medieval France."
    Comparative Literature Studies 32.2 (1995): 280-91.
    JSTOR. Web. 22 Sept. 2015.

Gravdal, Kathryn. *Ravishing Maidens: Writing Rape in
    Medieval French Literature and Law*. Philadelphia:
    University of Pennsylvania Press, 1991. Print.

Heaney, Seamus. *Beowulf: A Verse Translation*. Trans.
    New York, London: W.W. Norton & Company,
    2000. Print.

Hopkins, Amanda, Robert Allen Rouse, and Cory James
    Rushton, eds. *Sexual Culture in the Literature of*

Medieval Britain. Cambridge: D.S. Brewer, 2014. Print.

Karras, Ruth Mazo. *Sexuality in Medieval Europe*. New York: Routledge, 2005. Print.

Kelly, Michael J. "Christopher Marlowe and the Golden Age of England." *The Marlowe Society* 05. (2008): 1-30. Web. 22 Mar. 2016.

King James Bible. Chadwyck-Healey, 1996. Web.

Lees, Clare A. "Engendering Religious Desire: Sex, Knowledge, and Christian Identity in Anglo-Saxon England." *MLA International Bibliography* 27.1 (1997): 17-46. *The Journal of Medieval and Early Modern Studies* . Web. 21 Oct. 2015.

Leslie, Marina. "Incest, Incorporation, and King Lear in Jane Smiley's A Thousand Acres". *College English* 60.1 (1998): 31–50. Web. 22 March 2016.

Levine, Philip. *Saint Augustine: The City of God Against the Pagans*. Vol. IV. Cambridge, MA: Havard University Press, 1966. Print.

Levi-Straus, Claude. *The Elementary Structures of Kinship*. London: Eyre & Spottiswoode, 1969. Print.

Magiru, Anca. "Legal Archetypes in the Arthurian Legends: The Theme of Incest." *Journal of Research in Gender Studies* 4.2 (2014): 1110-4. *ProQuest.* Web. 4 Mar. 2016.

Malone, Kemp. *Studies in Heroic Legend and in Current Speech*. Copenhagen: Rosenkilde and Bagger, 1959. Print.

McCabe, Richard A. 1954- (Richard Anthony). *Incest, Drama, and Nature's Law, 1550-1700*. Cambridge University Press, 1993. Print.

McCabe, T. Mathew N. *Gower's Vulgar Tongue*. Cambridge: D.S. Brewer, 2011. Print.

McLaughlin, Megan. "Abominable Mingling: Father-Daughter Incest and the Law." *Medieval Feminist Newsletter* 24.Fall (1997): 26-30. Web. 16 Dec. 2015.

Marlowe, Christopher, 1564-1593. *Hero and Leander*. United States:, 1934. Web.

Malory, Sir Thomas. *Le Morte Darthur*. New York: Oxford University Press, 2008. Print.

Phelpstead, Carl. "The Sexual Ideology of "hrólfs Saga Kraka"'". *Scandinavian Studies* 75.1 (2003): 1–24.

Rosenblatt, Jason P. "Aspects of the Incest Problem in 'Hamlet'." *Shakespeare Quarterly* 29.3 (1978): 349-. Web.

Shakespeare, William. *Hamlet*. Oxford: Oxford University Press, 1992. Print.

Shakespeare, William. *King Lear*. New Haven, London: Yale University Press, 2007. Print.

Shakespeare, William. *Pericles*. London: Arden Shakespeare, 2004. Print.

Shepherd, Stephen H.A., ed. *Middle English Romances*. New York, London: W.W. Norton & Company, 1995. Print.

Symons, Victoria. "Commentary for Riddle 46." *The Riddle Ages*. Ed. Megan McCavell. N.p.

The Laws of the earliest English Kings. Trans. F. L. Attenborough. Oxford: Oxford University Press, 1922. *Hathi Trust*. Web. 30 Sept. 2015.

Taylor, Mark, 1939. *Shakespeare's Darker Purpose: A Question of Incest.* no. 7 Vol. AMS Press, 1982. Print.

Vines, Amy N. "Invisible Women: Rape as a Chivalric Necessity in Medieval Romance." *Sexual Culture in the Literature of Medieval Britain*. Ed. Amanda Hopkins, Robert Allen Rouse, and Cory James Rushton. Cambridge: D.S. Brewer, 2014. 161-80. Print.

Wolf, Arthur. Incest Avoidance and the Incest Taboos : Two Aspects of Human Nature. Palo Alto, CA, USA: Stanford Briefs, 2014. Print.

Richard J. Warren

About the Author

Richard J. Warren received his Bachelor and Master of Arts degrees in English Literature from the University of Nevada, Las Vegas. He is currently a Ph.D. candidate at the University of North Carolina, Greensboro.